FACT CAT

SEASHORE

Izzi Howell

WAYLAND

FACT CAT

Get your paws on this fantastic new mega-series from Wayland!

Join our Fact Cat on a journey of fun learning about every subject under the sun!

First published in Great Britain in 2015 by Wayland
Copyright © Wayland 2015

Wayland
An imprint of Hachette Children's Group
Part of Hodder & Stoughton
Carmelite House
50 Victoria Embankment
London EC4Y 0DZ

ISBN: 978 0 7502 8216 1
eBook ISBN: 978 0 7502 9470 6
Dewey Number: 333.9'17-dc23
10 9 8 7 6 5 4 3 2 1

Editor: Izzi Howell
Design: Rocket Design (E...
Fact Cat illustrations: Shu...
Other illustrations: Stefar...
Consultant: Kate Ruttle

Produced for Wayland by
White-Thomson Publishing Ltd
www.wtpub.co.uk
+44 (0) 843 208 7460

An Hachette UK Company
www.hachette.co.uk
www.hachettechildrens.co.uk

Printed and bound in China

Picture and illustration credits:
Dreamstime: jrstock 4, Vilainecrevette 8, Marco Lijoi 9, Deborah Coles 10 bottom, Rangizzz 14 top left, Pongphan Ruengchai top right; Shutterstock: gillmar cover, Mark Caunt title page, Darren Baker 5, Kathy Kay 11, Martin Fowler 12, Gabriele Maltinti 13 top left, Ron Rowan Photography 13 top right, Frank L Junior 13 bottom left, TTphoto 13 bottom right, Wesley Cowpar 14 bottom right, Tom Middleton 15, David Hanlon 16, marco mayer 17 top, Filipe B. Varela 17 bottom, Ed Samuel 18, EpicStockMedia 20; Thinkstock: photonaj 6, 7, Andy Piatt 10, rallinger_HH 14 bottom left, Fuse 19, 21.

Every effort has been made to clear copyright. Should there be any inadvertent omission, please apply to the publisher for rectification.

The author, Izzi Howell, is a writer and editor specialising in children's educational publishing.

The consultant, Kate Ruttle, is a literacy expert and ... hes in Suffolk.

FACT CAT FACT

There is a question for you to answer on each spread in this book. You can check your answers on page 24.

CONTENTS

WHAT IS A SEASHORE?

A seashore is an area where the land meets the sea or ocean. This **habitat** can be found all over the world, as most countries have seashores.

Seashores have rocks or sand. Find out what sand is made of.

sand

rock

Some seashores are next to high **cliffs**. Other seashores are by hills of sand, called sand dunes.

These sand dunes are made when the ocean wind blows sand off the beach.

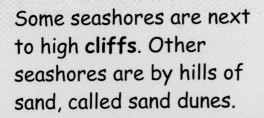

Canada has the longest seashore in the world. Its seashore goes around the east, north and west of the country and is over 200,000 km long.

HIGH AND LOW TIDE

Throughout the day, water from the ocean rises up on to the seashore and then falls away again. This movement of the ocean is called a **tide**.

At high tide, the water from the ocean rises onto the seashore. Most of the seashore is under water.

high tide

It takes about six hours for the tide to go in and come out again. Most seashores have two high tides and two low tides every day.

At low tide, the water moves away from the seashore. We can see the land that was under water during high tide.

low tide

ROCK POOLS

Rock pools are pools of seawater on rocky beaches. They are covered by the ocean at high tide. When the tide goes out, seawater stays in the rock pools.

Sea anemones don't have eyes. They use their **tentacles** to feel what is around them in the rock pool. Find out how many tentacles sea anemones have.

At low tide, sea birds look in rock pools for animals to eat. Small rock pool animals, such as hermit crabs, hide under stones and seaweed.

Hermit crabs don't have their own shells, like other crabs. Instead, they use shells other animals have left behind.

FACT CAT FACT

The word 'hermit' means a person who likes to be on their own. This isn't true for hermit crabs. They like to live in groups.

WILDLIFE

Many seashore animals, such as starfish, can only breathe underwater. However, if waves pull starfish onto the seashore, they can **survive** on land for a few hours until the next high tide.

If a starfish loses one of its arms, it can grow another arm in its place.

Sand dollars **bury** themselves under the sand to hide from other animals. Find out why they are called sand dollars.

The seashore is also home to birds, such as pelicans and seagulls. They build their nests on the beach, and catch food from the ocean.

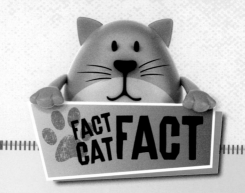

Seagulls drop animals with shells onto rocks to break them open. When the shell breaks, the seagulls eat the animal inside.

Pelicans use their **beaks** like a spoon to scoop fish out of the ocean.

PLANTS

Some seashore plants, such as bladder wrack, live underwater at high tide. They aren't covered by seawater at low tide.

Bladder wrack is a type of seaweed with tiny air pockets. If you squeeze the pockets, they will pop!

air pocket

Other seashore plants grow further away from the ocean, in sand or on rocks. These plants can survive in the strong wind and salty **spray** that come off the ocean.

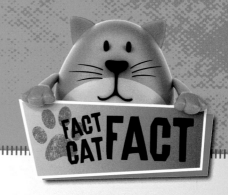

ice plant

silverweed

Ice plants and marram grass often grow on sand dunes. Find out which fruit comes from the ice plant.

marram grass

sea holly

A FOOD CHAIN

Seashore animals and plants get all their food from their habitat. Plants make their own food with the help of sunlight. Seashore animals eat plants or other animals.

Sunlight (makes food for)

Algae (eaten by)

We can use a food chain to see where animals and plants get their food from. Find out if humans can eat brown crabs.

Brown crab

Limpets (eaten by)

Food chains show us how everything is connected on the seashore. For example, brown crabs don't eat plants, but plants are still important to them. This is because brown crabs eat limpets, and limpets need plants to survive.

Seagulls eat many kinds of food, including starfish, insects and fruit.

FACT CAT FACT

Brown crabs don't walk forwards like most animals. They walk sideways because it is easier for them to move their legs this way.

FOOD FROM THE SEASHORE

Vegetables, such as marsh samphire, grow on the seashore. These are **wild** plants, so you shouldn't pick them if you want to try them. Instead, you can buy them in some grocery stores.

Marsh samphire tastes like salty asparagus. People often eat it with fish.

clam

mussel

We can find tasty shellfish, such as clams and mussels, buried in the sand or living on rocks. When you cook shellfish, their shells open and you can eat the meat inside.

If you are lucky, you might find a pearl inside a clam or a mussel. Find out the name of another animal that makes pearls.

pearl

VISITING THE SEASHORE

Some people visit the seashore for their holidays. There are many fun activities that you can do there, such as looking for shells or swimming in the sea.

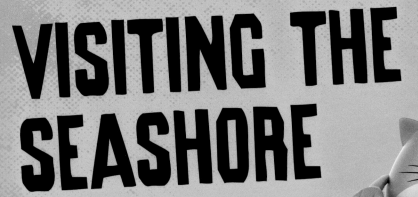

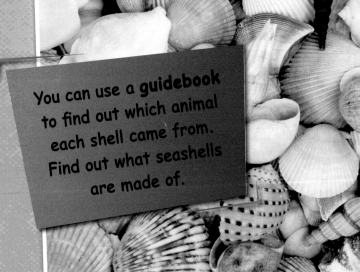

You can use a **guidebook** to find out which animal each shell came from. Find out what seashells are made of.

To keep safe in the ocean, you should always tell an adult where you are going and stay in **your depth**. Never go swimming if there are strong winds or high waves.

Lifeguards watch the ocean to make sure that no one is in danger.

PROTECTING THE SEASHORE

It is easy to **damage** the seashore, so you must be careful when you visit. If you pick anything up, put it back in the same place.

If you catch animals from rock pools, keep them in a bucket of water. Find out why you should use a net to catch seashore animals.

Some people leave rubbish when they visit the seashore. Rubbish from the ocean sometimes gets left behind after a high tide.

Rubbish can hurt or kill seashore animals if they eat it or get caught in it. By picking up rubbish from the beach, you can help **protect** this habitat.

FACT CAT FACT

We use more than one **trillion** plastic bags every year. A lot of these bags end up in the ocean or on the seashore, so try to use **reusable** bags instead.

QUIZ

Try to answer the questions below. Look back through the book to help you. Check your answers on page 24.

1 At high tide, most of the seashore is under water. True or not true?

a) true

b) not true

2 Rock pools are covered by water at high tide. True or not true?

a) true

b) not true

3 Pelicans build their nests on the ocean. True or not true?

a) true

b) not true

4 Brown crabs walk sideways. True or not true?

a) true

b) not true

5 In the past, people used seaweed as money. True or not true?

a) true

b) not true

6 It is fine to leave rubbish on the seashore. True or not true?

a) true

b) not true

GLOSSARY

beak the hard, pointy part of a bird's mouth

bury to put something in a hole in the ground and cover it

cliffs high, steep rocks near the seashore

damage to harm something

guidebook a book that gives you information

habitat the place where an animal or a plant lives

lifeguard someone who helps people if they are in danger in the water

nest a place where birds lay eggs and feed their young

protect to keep something safe

reusable something that you can use more than once before throwing it away

spray small drops of liquid blown through the air

survive to stay alive

tentacle a long part of a sea animal's body, similar to an arm

tide the regular change in the level of the water on the seashore

trillion one million million

wild growing naturally and not planted by humans

your depth the area in the ocean where your feet can touch the floor and your head is above the water

INDEX

ANSWERS

Pages 4–20

Page 4: Small pieces of rock

Page 6: Yes, they do, but they are too small for us to see

Page 8: Anywhere between ten and several hundred tentacles

Page 10: Because of their round shape – they look like a dollar coin!

Page 13: The sour fig

Page 14: Humans can eat brown crabs, in fact, they are also known as edible crabs

Page 16: Oysters

Page 18: Calcium carbonate

Page 20: Because it is easy to damage seashore animals with our hands

Quiz answers

1   true

2   true

3   not true, they build their nests on the seashore

4   true

5   not true, they used cowrie shells

6   not true, you should always pick up rubbish and put it in a bin

OTHER TITLES IN THE FACT CAT SERIES...

WAYLAND

SPACE

978 0 7502 8220 8

978 0 7502 8221 5

978 0 7502 8222 2

978 0 7502 8223 9

UNITED KINGDOM

978 0 7502 8433 2

978 0 7502 8440 0

978 0 7502 8439 4

978 0 7502 8438 7

COUNTRIES

978 0 7502 8213 0

978 0 7502 8212 3

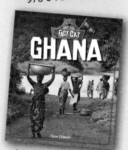

978 0 7502 8215 4

978 0 7502 8214 7

HISTORY

978 0 7502 9040 1

978 0 7502 9034 0

978 0 7502 9031 9

978 0 7502 9037 1